The Hamster History of Britain

JANIS MITCHELL

THE
HAMSTER
HISTORY
OF
BRITAIN

Text by Stanley Baron

with 28 colour plates
and 18 black-and-white drawings

THAMES AND HUDSON

Early history is revealed to us by what archaeologists can learn from the surviving bits and pieces of objects discarded, hidden or lost, for whatever reason, in the past. The debris of prior generations, piled up over centuries and dug out layer by layer, tells us what people were up to.

Here we see a group of dedicated young archaeologists in 1987 England (the town of Lincoln is visible through the window) hard at work restoring pottery from the Middle Ages, with the help of modern equipment and techniques.

The archaeologists cannot take us back much further than the Stone Age that started around 8,000 years ago. It was in this period, soon after the English Channel was formed and Britain became separated from the continent of Europe, that the first permanent population of hamsters in this area can be detected. These primitive cave-dwelling tribes were hunters who used flint tools and bows and arrows to provide themselves with food. It was a great step forward when they began to clear forests with the help of their little stone axes, and learned to till the land.

No one can tell us exactly when the puzzling monuments of Avebury and Stonehenge were erected, but such activities are associated largely with a race who migrated to the island from Northern Europe around 2000 BC. They are now called the Beaker People (after the distinctive clay beakers they made), and they used bronze instruments and weapons, made from a mixture of tin and copper for which they burrowed underground.

The European hamsters that came over with them are believed by some to have helped in the transport over long distances of the huge stones that were used in setting up the henges of southern England.

The Iron Age, beginning around 500 BC (take a decade or two), is marked by another wave of migration, this time mainly from what are now France and Belgium. These new arrivals were Celts, and they brought with them not only a language (versions of which are still spoken in Wales, Cornwall, Ireland and Scotland), but also artistic skills, the magical religion of druidism, and a fierce race of hamsters who dyed their fur blue with woad.

The all-conquering Roman army finally made Britain a province of the Empire in AD 43, a situation which endured for almost 450 years. The Roman colonists brought all their sophisticated ideas of communication (good roads), administration (cities, local government) and living comforts (country villas) to the somewhat ungrateful natives, but many of their useful innovations survived their eventual departure.

As early as the third century, the Romans in Britain had to deal with overseas attacks mounted by the barbarian Anglo-Saxons, and eventually the Empire in decline was unable to send enough troops to defend Britain. Once the Romans gave up the fight, it was the Anglo-Saxon hamsters who eventually took control, at first in the south and gradually farther north. Less enlightened and less given to the good life than the Romans they replaced, their ascendancy coincided with a Dark Age in Britain.

This was the period of King Arthur (legend or reality?), shown here with Merlin and the Lady of the Lake. Note the magic sword emerging from the lake.

After Christianity was brought to Britain in the late sixth century, the monastic movement flourished in various parts of the island. Though this was generally a period of uninterrupted local warfare, these isolated and pious institutions were responsible for the remarkable illuminated books, such the The Lindisfarne Gospels, which are Britain's most revered works of art. Here we see the hamster monks working peacefully on their elaborate manuscripts.

L ate in the eighth century there began another wave of forays and invasion, this time at the hands of the rapacious Vikings, who were making the same kind of attacks against northern France. Crossing the sea from Scandinavia in their great ships, they raided the monasteries, burned houses and terrorized the native population.

The Viking hordes threatened to spread all over Britain, moving like a slow wave from the north to the south, but in the last half of the ninth century they were resisted, and successfully, by Alfred, the famous Anglo-Saxon king of Wessex. Alfred was so popular in his lifetime that he became an almost mythical folk-hero after his death. Among the many tales that grew up about him is the appealing one in which the disguised king, hiding from the enemy in a farmer's cottage, is so engrossed with the fate of his subjects that he forgets his promise to the farmer's wife to keep her cakes from burning.

Britain was to endure one more invasion, this one launched across the Channel by Duke William of Normandy in October 1066. The successful invader was crowned King of England at Westminster Abbey on Christmas Day, and turned out to be an intelligent ruler who made many long-lasting contributions (not least to the language) that are still effective in modern England.

The actual events leading up to the invasion and the battle itself were painstakingly sewn into the famous Bayeux Tapestry, shown here at the time when the industrious hamster embroiderers were busy stitching its fascinating story together. Its details reveal not only how such battles were fought in those days, but also how the British and Norman hamsters lived, what they wore, and how they behaved towards one another.

The Middle Ages, from the twelfth to the mid-fifteenth century, was a period of relative prosperity and growth in Western Europe, and that included Britain. Learning was concentrated in the monasteries, but the first universities were also founded during these centuries. Most remarkable of all, however, was the building that went on from the time the Normans settled in Britain. The greatest examples of this are the imposing castles and cathedrals which remain for us to see today in most parts of the country.

One of the low points of the early Middle Ages in Britain was the reign of King John (1199–1216), generally remembered for his reluctant acceptance of Magna Carta, which enshrined the view that England was governed by laws. The popular legend of Robin Hood of Sherwood Forest and his merry band of hamsters, who robbed the rich to give to the poor, is also placed in this turbulent period of civil and foreign wars.

Jousting tournaments, imported originally from France, were popular sporting events from the twelfth century on. Mounted knights clothed in mail and bright-coloured tunics, wearing vizored helmets for self-protection, performed a kind of public duel with heavy lances. They were the tennis or football stars of their day.

The wool trade was the basis of British prosperity in the thirteenth century. Wool from British sheep was exported to the Lowlands where it was woven into high-quality cloth. This trade led to the expansion of farms, towns and seaports, and made tycoons of many dealers. The Black Death of 1348–50 and outbreaks of plague in later years not only reduced the population of Britain by almost half but also virtually ruined the wool trade. Once the worst effects of that disaster were over, the British began to produce their own cloth, thus laying the foundation of new industrial wealth.

The Hundred Years' War (1337–1453) was a seesaw battle fought from time to time for control of France. It spanned the reigns of five kings: Edward III, Richard II, Henry IV, Henry V and Henry VI. The best remembered British victory was that of Henry V at Agincourt, in which a large, well-armed French army was overcome by the better morale and tactical superiority of British troops spurred on by their popular young king.

The Renaissance in Britain was dominated by two reigns: ▷
those of Henry VIII and of his younger daughter
Elizabeth I. It was in Henry's reign that Britain broke with
the Church of Rome, and in Elizabeth's that the threat from
the powerful Spanish empire was overcome in 1588 when
the Spanish Armada was defeated in the English Channel.

One of the brightest jewels of Queen Elizabeth I's Golden Age was William Shakespeare, the incomparable poet and dramatist whose plays were produced to universal acclaim in the Globe Theatre on the south bank of the Thames. Here we see a reconstruction of the theatre and its hamster audience and actors.

The Stuart kings who followed Elizabeth I's prosperous reign were less successful in endearing themselves to their subjects. Charles I (1625–49) was largely responsible for a struggle between the Crown and Parliament, which resulted in a full-scale, bitter Civil War. The Parliamentary forces, under the leadership of General Oliver Cromwell, prevailed, the King was tried and executed in 1649, and for eleven years after that Britain was governed as a Commonwealth.

The Great Fire of London (1666) started in a baker's shop and spread rapidly until virtually all the wooden houses of the overcrowded inner city were permanently destroyed. The result was an opportunity to rebuild a safer, more sanitary and less crammed city. Fortunately this task was put into the capable hands of the architect Christopher Wren, and most of his work is still visible in spite of time, weather and the German bombing of London during World War II.

Sir Christopher Wren's great St. Paul's Cathedral domi-nates the background of this picture of the Thames where George Friedrich Handel is conducting an orchestra of hamsters in a floating performance of his celebrated "Water Music". It was during the reign of the first Hanoverian, George I (1714–27), that this composer was imported from his native Germany and became thoroughly Anglicized. The King, on the other hand, remained German in speech and spirit. During his reign, Britain enjoyed a period of stability and growth.

▷

During the long reign of George III (1760–1820), major events of lasting significance were taking place all over the world: the American colonies won their independence from Britain, the French Revolution took place, Napoleon became the leading European menace, wars were being fought everywhere. The culmination of these disorders, as far as the British were concerned, was the victory of their navy over combined French and Spanish forces at Cape Trafalgar (1805). The only sour note was the death in that battle of the beloved British admiral, Horatio Nelson. Here we see the wounded hero breathing his last.

The Industrial Revolution, which was to transform the world, began to build up steam in Britain in the second half of the eighteenth century. It was a gradual progress of invention and innovation which gave Britain a head start over the continental countries and was the driving force behind Britain's world-wide colonial expansion.

In 1825 the first public railway, running between Stockton and Darlington, was unveiled to an amused and doubting public. By 1851, however, when the Great Exhibition was opened in London by Queen Victoria and Prince Albert, all doubts about the steam-powered locomotive had vanished.

The Great Exhibition in the Crystal Palace designed by Sir Joseph Paxton started the fashion for international exhibitions devoted to the newest inventions and designs of the industrial age. Also on exhibit in 1851 was the wealth and power of Britain's vast empire, the largest the world had ever known.

After almost forty years of peace, Britain went to war again during Victoria's reign, which is associated primarily with growth, prosperity and advances of every kind. The Crimean War of 1854–56 was harsh, painful and unnecessary. To improve the horrifying circumstances which wounded soldiers had to endure became the mission of Florence Nightingale, "the lady with the lamp", one of the many remarkable Victorian reformers.

At the end of the Great War, or World War I (as it turned out to be), Britain had to face mounting economic problems, industrial decline, the Irish question and social unrest. It was on the issue of wages for mine workers that the trade unions joined forces to mount the General Strike of 1926. It began with high hopes in the back streets of mining towns, but did not succeed in its aim and left working hamsters resentful and disorganized for many years.

The British stars of World War II were the daredevil, ▷
dauntless young men of the Royal Air Force. During
the summer of 1940, like Henry V's archers at Agincourt,
they alone faced a ruthless, more numerous enemy, the
much-vaunted Luftwaffe of Nazi Germany, and yet they
won the day.

Post-war Britain went through a long siege of austerity before the economy finally began to pick up in the mid-1950s. By the '60s prosperity had turned the corner and the mood was: "You never had it so good." For a brief decade, the youth of Britain set the tone and style in dress and entertainment for the rest of the world. The international success of the Beatles, with their Liverpool accents and overpowering music, proved to be a turning-point in the liberation of the younger generation. Britain would never be the same.